AF382450

Maher Asaad Baker

Timeless Tales

ISBN Softcover: 978-3-384-32073-5

ISBN Hardback: 978-3-384-32074-2

ISBN E-Book: 978-3-384-32075-9

ISBN Large print: 978-3-384-32076-6

Cover image designed by Freepik

Contents

Introduction

Folk and historical myths have always been considered significant in the history of the world and they should concern today's inhabitants of the Earth.

It is thus clear that folktales have been in circulation for decades, and have equally entertained and terrified people at different epochs. For the greater part these mythological and epic stories with characters like gods, heroes and magical creatures were not mere repetitions of the thing in the ancient world. In the contemporary society, myths and legends are not perceived as significant with people relying on science. Even though as characters, they remain figments of the author's imagination, they are able to inform the reader on aspects such as human behaviour, morality, faith, and creativity.

As for the definition of the concept the myth and legends point to the traditional stories that are shot with the help of actors, with reference to the setting, and other aspects of the modern culture.

Myths are said to be traditional or epic stories that pertain to the historical past of a community or the events behind the existence of the phenomena in the natural world. Nearly all of them operate characteristics from super normal beings, persons, and other elements seen in religion and culture all over the globe. Myths are the popularised stories which are embedded in a chronological period considered before history or beginning of man. Some of them concern the beginnings of traditions and culture, faith and some of the characteristics of the environment.

There is a very thin line between deriving legends and myths but legends are concerned with the extraordinary skills of humans. Essentially, they are the types of narratives that history acknowledges but which do not hold steady ground, or else amorphous reiterations. As it has been noted earlier, legends have a nature of popularizing history events and turning such evident facts into stories that speak of heroes with unique abilities and outstanding performances. Other legends are mythological or completely invented but a search for the place has been made and a time is given.

Folk tales and myths have been practiced for thousands of years and are attributed to the preliterate communication where one generation passes the stories to the next generation of man. Myths that are defined as traditional stories that belonged to a certain society and introduced that society, explained how and why something began, why people started to do such things, how people died and what happened next, and who people were and what they were like in relation to the gods, were used to recount the beginning of the world and the beginning of man, the traditions of a certain culture and its rituals, and the occurrence and consequences of death. In the advanced manifestations of culture and literacy the myths and legends were written down in epics. For an instance, Homer's Iliad and Odyssey, Virgil's Aeneid, Epic of Gilgamesh, Norse, and the Hindu Vedas are regarded as epics that consist of myths of a given culture.

Myths and legends served several vital functions in ancient cultures:Many of the myths and legends played several important roles in ancient societies as follows:

- Explain Natural Phenomena: The myths were probably giving descriptions on natural phenomena that early societies perhaps could not probe into scientifically for instance, sunrise, seasons, weather, geographical features and life and death. It provided people with solace since it was believed that unjustified outcomes in nature's behavioral evidences were the manifestation of gods; thus, people were relatively less hopeless while watching the destruction.

- Validate Cultural Practices: These mythologies were hence employed by various cultures to explain why they practiced what they implemented, their behavior and even the social setup they put in place. Myths came in to explain or complete what science and knowledge did not provide answers to ; for instance why people went through a rite of passage, why is the world controlled by men and not women? The has however, brought about a feeling of belonging as well as an assigned responsibility to the people.

- Provide Moral Guidance: Often the myths show the consequences of such sins as pride, behaving evil and performing evil actions and disobedience to Gods while virtues are more often punished: courage, generosity , willingness to die for others and the like ; it showed the ancients how Gods conceived people should act or should not act.

- Explain the Unknown: They provided accounts of how and why things happened and responded to questions which even in the modern world give hard=time to respond to, the questions that are; what happens when one dies, the formation of the universe, creation of people and other questions for which there were no answers. Most cultures have myths relating to afterlife and creation despite the difference in the type of cultures. Thus, these stories offered people a shield against the unknown and, consequently, gave them security and tranquility.

- Transmit Tradition and History: Because early people did not have an opportunity to write, they passed the knowledge necessary for the successful survival of the next generation in the form of stories and myths. Here, the ancients were in a position to impart the said information from one generation to the other without the help of writing but with the help of narratives.

- Provide Entertainment: Folk had received myths and legends from poets and bards who enacted the tales, emotions and all, before there was television and books. We understand that fairy tales were even more developed and the listeners were entertained in the same way, today's movies entertain by the camp fire. The other roles of the myths were perhaps more important, but fun was definitely not one of them.

Therefore, observing these shows individuals might get the impression that myths, legends have no role to play in today's society.

Today's people in general can in no way regard such stories as real stories about the sky and the earth. However, mythology still plays an influential role in the modern world in the following ways: Thus, mythology cannot be considered to be unimportant in the contemporary world in the following aspects:

1. It is also required to enlighten the students concerning previous beliefs and culture.

The myths are essential for the modern society because they enable people to understand how the ancient civilizations treated life and the world that people could be confined to before scientific methods where brought into the picture. About the techniques that the early people used in their thinking, the values that they employed and the whole process of their belief system myths offer an understanding. They depict the cultural similarities and differences over time and between different societies that are relevant even up to date. Realizing that such notions, using at least one example, are inherited from ancestors makes people describe their similarity.

2. Informatively impacting Modern Sociology and Psychology

Both Carl Jung and Joseph Campbell were philosophers and thinkers and they both tried to study myths of all societies and cultures and concluded that all the symbols and all the archetypes are derived from the collective-unconsciousness. It may be concluded here that it is possible to explain certain patterns like such the hero's journey and keep thinking that they are embedded universally as, in fact, they often originate in the subconscious level. Thus, myths continue the tradition of indicating that the Africans of the present age have the same soul issues, questions, and search for identity and meaning as the ancestors, although they, perhaps, inhabit different material environments. Particularly, myths are the most striking an influential type of narrative because they give one an understanding of the essential constituents about one being and make one consider the holding principle in the given society.

3. Appreciating Literature and Art

Tales are a genre in art that began even from the ancient times and has been integrated in literature, poetry, as well as the visual arts till present days. Myths are universal experiences in the sense that it contains aspects that were timeless, and so, writers and artists have redefined these characters and symbols into a myth that modern individuals and artists can experience because myths are part of today's world. Whether it is in Shakespeare's play, other play/movies like epic fantasy or Star Wars or any movie based on myth one is able to make out and enjoy the moves.

4. The Religious and Moral Training and Development

Even today, information from myths offers legal guidelines, knowledge, equity plus divine help, which people continue to seek. Knowledge such as myths about the creation of the world, gods' contact with the communities and fables of ethical man are still helpful in the Formation of an individual character and the society. Therefore, mythology makes it possible to merge the recognisable secular spirituality within life and the view of such truths and values which exist beyond all of us. It is still significant to have the driving force of seeking meaning in learning from the elders throughout the days when people do not take the myths or the gods seriously any longer.

5. Thus, Hoff paved the way for future children's entertainers in the wake of the '70s and continued to create new episodes of the show, offering a unique approach to the showmanship and capturing the hearts of more generations.

Before wrapping it up, it is essential to notice that myths and legends make people happy through fabulous beasts, wonder, main characters giants, otherworldly locations, and offer an opportunity to escape to another world as it mostly is the case with genre in the majority of cases that are associated with fantasy and science fiction. Often, the ability to close one's eyes and let the imagination fly over interesting, even exotic, regions is a joy in life and a cure for worry. The love that people have towards the myths of old and the amazing tales of the Gods and Goddesses is something that fits the definition of completely satisfying. And things such as evil and the triumph over it, and such are general, and thus aids in the uniting people regardless of the tales they listen to. At this point, they want to convey that no matter how society, civilization, technology, and so on advance, the main factors that can add happiness to people's lives remain elementary – magic and imagination.

However, to the present day mythology remains an indispensable element of individual's life while it originates in the epoch little having relation to the scientific and technical one. Fort besides myths depict personality and psychology of the ancestors and, therefore, they are more than just explanations of the phenomenon in question and, so long as one is interested in myths as bearing social truths about oneself, they are still true. But the myth imagination is still the source of the most incredible stories and marvelous creations in literature, experience of religion and merely fun for people. People still tell myths because, paradoxically, myths are a way of providing an account to people regarding who and what they are as people and useful in the attempt of sorting information while also prophylactically preserving that information's mystery.

Mythological Foundations

Folk tales have remained to be one of the oldest friend of culture as recorded in the history of man. Myths are actual and traditional stories of gods and spirits, heroes, and other rather marvelous and extraordinary events that have been narrated and passed down ; the myths of the society inculcating the belief, values, culture and even purpose of life from the generation that created it. One is able to understand that myths were the way through which our ancestors in different parts of the world undertook to explain to the outsiders the kind of thoughts, creativity as well as practices they had as well as their perception on the universe.

The gods of Olympus and mythical stories with the heroes are still some of the most recalled and realised traditions left behind by the ancient people. These are the pleasurable stories of vying for power, sibling rivalry, love and envy, retribution, voyage, and salvation which are felt to this day. As for me, it's the relevance of the source materials; it can be definitely stated that it is due to the talents of the original storytellers and, of course, the eternal thirst of the human spirit to find its reflection in the Mirror of Myth.

Divine power, gods and goddesses,magical creatures, spirits and demons or evil powers were other contributors to mythology in Ancient Greece. Its head was Zeus of the kings when, after the Olympians defeated the Titans, the brothers and sisters displaced one another. They shaped him to be a leader endowed with the ability of brightening the storm; as an extension, he had the equivalent of the lightning and thunderbolt, and since he suffered from mood swings, he was, therefore, erratic. Zeus was the king of the Universe, yet other gods still oversaw sections of life; Aphrodite was the goddess of beauty while Dionysus watched over the vineyards, Hephaestus over the smelters. Mythologies appear in mortal's existence acting as gods and goddesses in aspects such as warring, battling in tournaments, in prophesying, gift bestowing and even in romantic affairs with mortal lovers.

But the Greek mythology told also great heroes and significant and essential myths. Poems like the 'Illiad' and 'Odyssey' therefore have the function of narrating events and or cultural values, for instance, Achilles fighting the Trojans and or Odysseus trying to get back home. They also give one the power to visualize and ponder over some such human virtues as pride, anger, love, sorrow and will power. However such sociocultural myths do provide rather shy glimpses into the early human consciousness.

Last but not the least, anthropomorphism, cosmopsychism, logos, mythos, and pathos fabricated a rich and complex cosmological paradigm and parable and epic myth for the Greeks. These sorts and archetypes persist to this date as the basis of creative adaptations of more generations in relation to these primary narrative components upon which the construction of the Western civilizational structure was made.

While in the framework of the Greek mythology the gods and goddesses gathered in Olympus and became a single oppressive governing body all at once, the Nordicism had many more and superordinate levels in its universe. The gods of the ancient Greeks and Romans were far from being perfect and even could be sinful; superior giants, hurtful enchanters, great warriors, mischievous and ill-natured chimeras, wise and evil magicians, frightening shadows, and many others gods and other superhuman beings. It was created with the central room of the great hall of Valhalla and was managed with the one-eyed main god Odin. However the basic tree Yggdrasil was drawn located in the middle of the universe which connected the fire with the ice, the gods with the men.

It speaks of gods emerging from the dead body of Ymir, the giant, to form a new universe, the hammer Mjolnir given to Thor, the god of thunder, by the dwarves, Aesir's wars against other gods, and the Ragnarok that ends the world. Knowledge is presented as the main motivation of the characters since gods, giants and humans all strive to find out the information they need to change their destinies. But what we get to see in the fairy tale/legendary context are rather primitive instincts – Thor's anger, Freya's passion, Loki's jealousy. Although not as dominant in modern culture as Greek myths are, Norse stories influenced the European traditions and folk tales. Sounds still linger in the form of folklore and creatures such as the vampire along with other terminologies like 'Ragnarok', 'Valkyrie', and 'Mjolnir'.

Norse sagas make existence in the world to be composed of being opposite, being together, being betrayals, being punished, and being reconciled due to transportations of gods, giants, humans, and creatures. As with all oral narratives, the ideas remain with one long after the details are forgotten – and thus it was with the stories of Ancient Greece. Such copious examples from these primeval narratives explain how mythology assists mankind in dealing with the existential concern and challenges of existence, existence's purpose, cohabitation, and absolutes, and annihilation.

Religious beliefs of Ancient Egypt played a significant role in culture preserving the god-king system and obeying the idea of cosmic justice. One of the characteristics of Egyptian mythology unlike Greek or Norse that were replete with stories of battling gods, was the limited presentation of antagonism between gods. The fight against chaos in humanities history involved virtually all 'major' gods of the Egyptian pantheon, except a few deities with more or less ambiguous status, and the pharaoh who was considered to rule by divine right, into a fairly coherent administrative structure.

As less aggressive towards each other as compared to Norse or Greek gods, Egyptian gods took a lots of animalistic and anthropoid transformations in Egyptian art and mythology. Bastet transformed itself into a cat and Anubis into a jackal headed god whenever they had to show the souls their fate in the afterlife. While Osiris held the throne of the dead, Ra was the one to traverse the heavens. Some of the many goddesses include Isis, and the following shows the authority bestowed upon the goddesses. Myth-associated gods were worshipped by performing rituals that aimed at ensuring that the gods bestowed the community and especially the royalty with abundance, good health and success.

Thus, besides confirming the social order, myths inspired the Egyptians to learn morality and spirituality. For example, the myth of Osiris offers an earlier introduction to knowledge about death and rebirth The myth, over decadent emotions of joy, expresses the constant battle of light against darkness – myths regarding the sun god 's nightly battle against demons during his journey through the underworld. Such stories re-emphasized such cultural perspectives as just leadership, civil order, and the ephemeral nature of life.

Compared to myths from some other pantheons, Egyptian legends have not been as present in modern culture worldwide as they have been for thousands of years influencing neighboring cultures. This fact is indicative of the fact that mythology is a transmission of archetypal issues, such as the ones we have just seen, that people have sought to answer across the ages.

Aside from the mythologies of the ancient Egyptians, Greeks, and Norse, other mythologies cropped up in other parts of Africa, Asia, Oceania, and the two Americas. There is not much difference as they are synchronized in every society and harmonize with each culture's historical background, their beliefs, the ideas of their philosophies, and their cosmologies. For example, the stories involving gods fighting with prehistoric adversaries in artistic or destructive struggles, multilevel worlds, intelligent and cunning deities and spirits, and the concept of the struggle between duality – the world of order and chaos, the flood that clears the face of the earth before the creation of man.

This is where it is necessary to mention that African mythology combines thousand of ethnic lore while at the same time sharing the elements inherent to most of the world's mythological systems , the trickster spirits, deities who establish the link between the heaven and the earth and are a repository of the breath of life in the human race. Many myths are the chronicles of how different things in the world and its attributes came into existence, there are cosmogonic myth as well as definition of what constitutes vice and virtues in the society. In epics people combat with arbitrary gods or spirits and narratives and songs are conventionalized in many societies with proverbs. 'These are deities and in most often portray gods as half human and half animal or just simply an object with a natural or celestial form.'

There is the cast of gods, heroes of superiority, marvelous monsters and manifold philosophies in Asian mythology. Indian mythology developed a large number of

Shadow histories for other gods, for example Vishnu and Ganesha with the traditions told in Ramayana, Mahabharata, Vedas and Puranas. Stakeholders in Chinese culture relayed mythological and folklores about accounts like Xia or Shang dynasties or inclusive of moral lesson that was encompassed in the accounts. That is why many myths begin with something like a cosmogonic egg that has a god in it or distinguish between the creativeness of dragons and the destructiveness of floods. Japanese Shinto mythology particularly deals with the Kamis, they are spirits which are inherent in certain natural items, animals, large pieces of land and people.

A myth gives indigenous people intimate relation to the ground, a peculiar outlook of the world, and strength that the traditions offer; at the same time, when acknowledging the stories behind them, people appreciate the mythologies. For example, in Native American mythology the gods are given the role of being the keepers of game, plants and water, fire, and lightning and rain as well are noted to be the protectors of humanity. Big creator gods during the dream time and correlation of geographical features of a region with their mythology can be illustrated by the Australian Aboriginal oral traditions. These mythic stories and their moral lessons are relevant even to this day for the First Nations bands and tribes that are still passing the lore.

Together this is the global picture of mythology in the world which depicts that mythology is common to all human beings but there are regional flavors. In the very process of developing myths to answer the questions of existence, explain the surrounding world, set norms, and establish social relationships, there are certain lines that, while unraveled to fit specific geography, persons, difficulties, and perspectives, manifested themselves as cultural universal archetypes. Myths will very probably go on telling the story of the human condition and telling it to humanity as long as, to the audience of the latest generations, the tales are conveyed as the eternal values.

Significance

Myths, legends and folktales – these grand-scope historical narratives of both heroes and gods, mythical beings and monsters have been told as far as man's race could go back in history. Discredited in the present ages as myths and histories, mythology in the contemporary world has remained a force that instills dreams and creates cultures. Secondly, myths are entertaining in that they reflect the subconscious behaviors, values, and tendencies of people, give weighty ontological patterns, and bring human beings together.

That is why it is important to look for myths' connection to the mind, the existential theme, and the community, to outline why such stories are still meaningful at the present moment.

Myths portrayed in this book can be explained by the insight of psychology to explain how myths are consistent in regard to periods in which they are written. For instance, it is possible to discuss Carl Jung and his theories about archetypes of the collective unconscious that he discovered in myths and their stories. And as people themselves are not born colour-blind, or stupid, or with some sexual perversion, but are born with some phobia, for example, phobia of snakes or with some definite character, the same they are born with some definite predisposition to some images and some stories. These psychological dispositions are the basis of myths which contain forms for the entire human race.

The Hero's Journey archetype shows the connection between myths and mental inclinations that existed in the ancient culture: As defined by the scholar Joseph Campbell, the most basic mythos is the monomyth, or cycle of the hero, with characteristics of the departure, the initiation, and the return. As it was described in many legends, including Odyssey, at the core it is a legend of a single person who leaves a home and has to face opponents, gets a reward/power and changes the final process of returning home. It assumes a cyclic structure of the story, which specifies one of the most universal plots of the word culture identification – to obtain power and knowledge in a foreign country to help one's people afterward. The essence of the phenomenon lying in every person is characterized in the structures of myths stating that the Hero's Journey is a definite mission which means the state of constant development and self-actualization as well as providing help to people.

In this connection there is nothing remarkable in the fact that myths also embody primitive emotions. Divinity can lose its temper and behave in such a manner, get inflamed by love and do things out of pride or any other basic instinct. Such fears as the dark, death, and ritual pollution that were described in traditional vaguer figures such as the dragon and the demon. Such feelings are projected into myths and thus delivering to the people a myth which serves to mirror the distinct psychological processes. For instance, *Orpheus, who could not bring back Eurydice* is also connected with mourning as something dear is lost to us. Myths provide hypothetical locales where people's phantasies can be enacted, and the processes of interiorization and emoting can occur. The elements of the fantastic thus enable the access to feeling facts.

Thus, whether they are built up in the fashion of the typical Hero Journeys or drenched in emotion as these myths are, people through the millennia have fixed their interest on myths because they touch deep down certain psychological processes and ways of handling stress. They do not present tedious amusements ; they present visions of things that are Psycologicsal and permanent in mankind.

Therefore, myths not only reveal psychological aspects of the world but also express a vision of the philosophy of this world. Therefore, the mythic plot shows visions on what concerns the last issues in the existence, for example, the structure of the universe and the ways a person has to live as if it – cosmological forces as the characters or representation of the effects of choices. It can be fairly suggested that myths as work of philosophy represent a separate category of philosophical discourse which indeed played a great role in shaping thoughts in people during centuries.

Cosmogony, or creation and structuring of the world, is a part of philosophizing that is associated with myths. For instance, as the Norse mythology describes, the giant known as Ymir was the first identified giant to be defeated by gods Odin, Vili and Ve and thereafter killed and out of his remains the new world was fashioned. On it he makes his flesh his ground, his blood — his seas, his bones these hills. This myth describes the cosmogony of the subsequent world from a murdered first born giant. It creates the preconditions for divine order in which gods reign over the spheres of mortal which they inhabit. Paradigms are also depicted by myths like a Wake up call design where meanings are negotiated in order/against chaos and/or purity/against defilement. In order to emphasize that myths show how the world and people are arranged referring to characters and actions, defining philosophical orientations of people, it is necessary to note that myths denote existence and nature of the world utilizing characters and incidents.

Myths also solve philosophical issues of how one is supposed to live a good and virtuous life due to the application of parables. According to a Cameroonian myth there is one Mbuma travelling and meeting a boy who is a shape-shifter turning into a dove then a turtle then a buffalo. In the words of an unknown author, every being is endowed with some wisdom; birds are wise because they have no hesitation in calling for a flight; similarly buffaloes are wise because they do not rush for anything and are sensible enough to do things leisurely, step by step. From these transformations, the aspects of Mbuma is given a practical approach on how to appreciate the diverse paradigms. This story is a paradigm that has illustrations which are suggested through the story as ideas of philosophy on flexibility and balance whereby this is an advocacy of how myths influence activity through stories.

The third philosophical area that has regularly been dealt with in myths is that of mortality.

The Epic of Gilgamesh shows kings searching for immortality after his friend Enkidu dies, accurately capturing the idea of mortality's and loss. In Norse myth even ruling gods such as Baldr dies thus illustrating the fact that even the super natural creatures undergo death. Nevertheless, contemplating this death anxiety directly, myths also provide the psychological reward of individuation by promoting posthumous, immortal fame through the writing of poets. Myths thus study very mortal endeavors to find a sense as long as there is death. This philosophical role still remains relevant in the modern world as a source of comfort and reflection on the transient nature of life.

Thus, from painting a cosmos to defining ethical norms to addressing death, myths offer play out complex philosophical narratives that address concerns that are otherwise difficult to express in a plain narrative. It is where characters and creativity become crucial to philosophy to contain the mythic storytelling that has the ability to sketch the absolute paradigms of the world and existence.

So, there are social dimensions of meaning beyond psychological and philosophical currency of myths. They also provide the necessary means of establishing and enforcing group cohesion and moralities without which any given society cannot thrive. If even as literal truth claims myths provide traditional referents for what in a society coheres, let alone the more profound metaphysical and epistemological truths that have been revealed?

Another social function of myths is the process of making a cultural definition. In particular, origin myths set up idealized genealogical relations that define how a given group regards things and behaves. For instance, the myths of origin of Ancient Sparta focus on couples passing through arduous military tests. which in turn supports cultural characteristics of militarism and toughness. Ervard, myths provide a common story that gives meaning to why rituals were created in the first place, thus providing social function via the symbolism.

In addition, myths have a purpose of informing people in right or wrong behaviors through characters' portrayals. Inanna descends to the lower world: The myth of Inanna and the descent of the underworld that is all about the Sumerian goddess Inanna's descent into the lower world to visit her husband, is a myth that describes all the proper procedure to cross the lower world appropriately. Her passage also sets a godly example on how people especially daughters should bury their dead. Inanna however encounters her sister Ereshkigal the counterpart of her father's wife, the deity of the underworld who becomes the wife of the usurper in an attempt to save her husband from the depths of the pit. This aggressive action is inapplicable based on the interpersonal codes, and thus, Inanna is killed.

In another case, she is only revived in case her servant observes certain procedures of pleading for mercy. Reflected in this regard, the result of the myth, thus, defines the social ethics as to the roles of populating rebellion or conforming among them. The fantastic drama present real moral tendencies and the ways how people should behave in front of others.

They also create people's togetherness through association since people have to amalgamate in order to be in a position to practice what is deemed to be associated with myths. Myths in rituals: such things as translating festivals to gods, dramatic restaging of epics or the myths told by a shaman round the campfire are manifestations of how myths integrate a society. Here they first recognize other people and the whole history of the society through the ritualization of the stories. This establishes togetherness not only in terms of the information that can be obtained from myths but also in several other aspects as well.

Why, myths are no longer myths if literally interpreted as history, as some of these books discussed earlier have shown it. In the same way science reduces stars or evolution as a less believable source of stars or infact makes the physical make of the biblical story of Eden less real, myths are taken away from the position of being true history or even physical history. However, their symbolism and ideology are still seen up until the present. The findings of myths include signs, figures, and mutual affiliations that are still logically necessary to define group cohesion and mission.

It can be therefore said that the myth is a strategy of social incorporation or constitution of identity, the conveyance of the socially normative or appropriate behavior and the construction of an archival practice. And so when claims of mythology decrease, culture 'holding' remains the case.

To assert that the agents from myths and fabulous actions have always impressed the human beings is not a chance at all. Thus the myths embody inner attitudes of the individual in forms which are objectively present in singular pictures, unforgettable figures and distinctly shaped images. Cosmogonic myths depict the events at the dawn of existence, give people guidelines of right and wrong actions, and set reference points for social structures. Therefore, while the myths being associated with the supernatural world evoked through the application of reason in archaic societies has somewhat been vanishing with reason and science, the psychological outlook, the philosophy to be pursued and the societal role that is required cannot be removed.

The poet Muriel Rukeyser said myths are "the traces of the visions of people setting out to answer the questions: Questions suggested by existentialism include 'Who am I? What is the purpose of my life'? These questions can resonate through the universe and across the ages, because they touch on the very fundamentals of human life. Myths constitute an attempt to create definitive images for the intricate strictures of man's heart and then impose them together in figures that may be collectively shared to render the world and our roles comprehensible. As long as the questions of meaning are with the people, myths will continue to shed meaning through presenting similar people, explaining the universe, and stabilizing society's framework. For all the deities might crumble, the domain of myth is perpetually an invite to reach out for the significance of one's existence.

Contemporary Cultural Reinterpretation

Since the dawn of the use of writing by man, myths and legends have been there and have always been included in arts and culture. These are the great myths and legends of gods, heroes, mythical beasts and the supernatural which has remained relevant down the ages as folklore which tells the emotional essence of people of various generations with the constantly renewed plot and moral that needs to be addressed by the new generations. Such retries are a process constant and evidently confirm the major role of myths and legends in the society, and as the material for modern manufacture, versatility of myths.

I think that one can easily identify many authors who have dealt with the Realization of the myth and other archetypes discovered in world literature and enriched the text with new and estimative ideas and concepts. The need for 'New' old fables in the epoch of postmodern writing assists in the methodical dismantling of mythical models, the plausibility of a psychological realist aesthetics, problems of ethics, and the transmutation of myths into philosophical allegories.

Subgenres that appear to use a great deal of mythopoietic speculation and seem to be replete with mythic reiterations are the Genres of fantasies and sci-fi subgenres. Fantasy literature and languages' master J.R.R. Tolkien employed a lot of architectural elements adopted from the Norse and Germanic mythologies to build the geography of his Middle-earth and populate it with different-natured races including the elves, dwarves and orcs. This person also applied some aspects of Celtic folklore and therefore provided halflings with some of them. Tolkien's close friend C. S. Lewis employed Greek and Roman myths, and Christian motifs in his the chronicles of Narnia, a children's book.

When having to tell a similar fabula, other modern authors of fiction in the genre of fantasy, such as Neil Gaiman, bring an interesting and socially responsible spinning of a feminist and coming-of-age subplot, which can be observed in works like American Gods and The Ocean at the End of the Lane. In addition, it can be stated that Star Wars movies show the myths set the framework of the whole sci-fi structures. For his galaxy, far far away George using aspects from different cultures and put stereotypical characters such as the warrior maiden, the mystical old man and the cinder fella hero.

That is not limited to the prose but also to the improvement of the myths in the genre of poetry and drama as well. W.B. Yeats the poet of the Nobel prize wrote meditations on one of the legends of Ireland – Cuchulain, a hero in the fight against invasion and the embodiment of national selfishness which fights against the penetration of civilization. T.S. Eliott, a contemporary of yeats is another writer who did search for solace in mythical framework in his most famous piece.- The Waste Land where he interferences the fragments of chronicle of the Fisher king which has social message in it.

In the sphere of theatre the French existentialist philosopher and playwright Jean-Paul Sartre adapted an existentialist play called The Flies which has roots in Greek myth Oresteia, the events of the play occur during the German occupation of France.

Thus, like Gide before him, with the help of putting the story in the context of the Greek tragedy and focusing the audience's attention at the choice, Sartre implicitly urged French to defy the Germans and make the 'impossible' ethical choice. Such kinds of transformations are good examples of the literature through which famous mythic stories narrated in childhood can be repeated.

Some authors chose to alter the story to a minimal level and preserve myths as the primary genre of the work while altering the perception towards the story. Finally, the Penelopiad by Margaret Atwood follows the common idea but is postmodern, as it is based on Penelope's perspective of the events. Thus, Penelope is a character taken from Homer's epic yet she does not fit the mold of the submissive, loyal wife of the Odyssey stereotype but the overall legend is recalled.

The wise King Arthur has been a subject of interpretation for all the tales to be transferred to every other story. For instance, The Once and Future King by T. H. White, which describes the process of King Arthur's rise to power through illustrations of Camelot as people's desire to establish a haven in the middle of war as a plot. It is therefore not surprising that again and again, very familiar mythic topography is called into service for redevelopment.

From painting to sculpture, but comics, to film and television, the myths as a source of inspiration dominate the twentieth century. gods and heroes continue to be part of the armature and are painted and acted out with the purpose to show the aspects of different cultural situations like in the different time periods.

Some of the things that people like to see in paintings and sculpture include:Some of the things that people like to see in paintings and sculpture include:

Greek, Norse and Celtic mythology have been presented with fabulous gods and goddesses that have given countless pleasures to the fine artists of terrific generations. Thus, while the main goal of this particular study was to focus on the analysis of Picasso's paintings, it can be stated that the artist often depicted the classical myths in the style of modernism throughout the years of his activity. Thus, the changes to the socially known representations of mythical characters as painted experiments led to the cubism to be acknowledged by the culture and hence to the abstractions.

Another surrealist painter, is Salvador Dali who associated myths that are depicted in the hot, bright images of nightmares. Consequently, paintings such as The Metamorphosis of Narcissus are suggestive of his general interpretation of gothic surrealism by rehearsing ancient fables. The neoclassical movement sculptors for instance Claudel,

Rodin, and Leighton were engaged in figurative works of bronze and marbles, and they intended to portray gods and heroes.

It can be noted that the type of myths that have prolix and lavish details which appear in form of episodes suits the genre of graphic narrative. For instance, in the traditions of American comics they have such characters as 'superheroes' which in actual fact are super beings, today's Gods, enchanters, people with God like qualities and powers. Comparing heroes to gods is not impossible – characters like Superman or Wonder Woman have their divine origin identifiable, all their divine traits are quite obvious Stan Lee just took mythological tales and brought them into modern essence by creating heroes like

Spiderman or the X-Men – the fights of the hero with the society, with the world, his outcast status, his preordained fate – all are reminiscent of fights of legends.

A number of grand graphic novel adaptations of myths are effortful, and here Neil Gaiman's Norse Mythology where is an effective, stately, and innovative re-imagining of the most renowned and vigorous Nordic myths as gripping comic books. Much more appalling is the award-winning series; The Wicked + The Divine by Kieron Gillen illustrated by Jamie McKelvie where gods are portrayed similarly to pop stars which are considered as materialistic hedonists of the modern society.

Staying with the great cinematographic art and inspiration by mythology of creation of the spectacular and fantastic stably remains the main result. The legends of such things that can be seen on the big cinema screens, for instance, the fleece of gold or a complex mission of the character named Jason whom everybody knows is translated into space operas such as star wars telling about the passive or rather simply ignorant hero – Luke skywalker – who searches for the guidance attributed to unknown masters. Arguably some of the Celtic and Nordic myths are in the framework of Peter Jackson's live action adaptations of J.R.R Tolkien and the Thor feature films.

To make a conclusion, the authors of such television shows as mythology as if it were real life, for example, reveal the contemporary relevance of myths. Horrible series like Game of Throne tell the romance of the Medieval America and the Vikings' brutality. Preteen animated shows offer more comical explanations, which to an extent is observed in the Disney Hercules movie and the corresponding cartoon series where myths are translated into ridiculous circumstances. And Mythic Quest of Apple TV+ again repeats the fundamentals of the hero's path and at the same time making fun of the entire metanarrative set in the backdrop of game creators. In any case, myths are seen to be the means of leaving a trace in media no matter the approach and strategy introduced.

That is why myths indicate to us the world in general and appeal to the instincts which are eternal. But it would be little wonder then that it has been embraced in all types of musical instrumentation, from the full classical orchestra to the rock hit music bands today. As many of the music artists are able to successfully relay the more symbolic and emotional aspects of myths into their compositions, they discover new and deeper ways of passion within the work.

The composers of the classical era recognized myth as one of the major external source that they had at their disposal at any point of time. One of the most powerful and monumental instances of getting to work with the myths connected with the Northern and Germanic cultures is the list of works by Richard Wagner in particular the tetralogy which is based on the German mythological network – Der Ring des Nibelungen or The Ring of the Nibelung – the mythic music drama per excellence. Contemporary and appropriate forms of provocation are easily detected through the examples of Igor Stravinsky's 'The Rite of Spring' – a ballet and orchestral concert which also caused a great deal of scandal due to the actual slaughtering of a maiden dancer in a rather heathen spring ceremony.

Mythic elements are also present although less obvious in other nontroversial works from the classical period such as Debussy's music

Prelude to the Afternoon of a Faun which has its root from a Greek pastoral poem. Opera still provides new adaptations of myths to the stage as present-day operas such as the Finnish composer Kaija Saariaho's Emilie about the life of a well-known mathematician Émilie du Châtelet. Such offerings only demonstrate that audiences to this day are eager to sit with their eyes glued to the screen while mythic stories unfold to rousing instrumental music.

Other popular genres that have time and again employed myths as source of potent themes include hard rock, folk rock and art rock musicians. Heavy metal icons Led Zeppelin engaged with occultism and Tolkenian fantasy, which starts with controversy in the fourth album "Battle of Evermore" and "Stairway to Heaven" symbolism based on Norse mythology British singer Kate Bush loves romance and heartbreak, as seen in her works like "Cloudbusting" and "And Dream of Sheep" set against the backdrop of the Celtic.

By taking the audience on tightly orchestrated mythical journeys, the concept albums such as the American rock band The Decemberists folk influenced record 'The Hazards of Love'. This sometimes led to criticism of sensationalism or even of posturing of the authors as myths were employed as a source of inspiration. However, at their finest, the mythic quality of rock and pop contains the elemental allure of contemporary epic poets.

Musical theater is also the most appropriate representational form for mythic material, given the former's imaginative scope and emotional amplified nature. Hadestown: The Myth Reimagined On Broadway, Instrumental Singer-Songwriter Anaïs Mitchell's runaway Broadway hit, Hadestown is a musical of Orpheus' quest for Eurydice in the Underworld with a folk-steampunk twist. The musical also achieved the same level of critical acclaim and fan base with the help of depicting gods as relatable human characters – especially with faults, such as lonely Hades, or moody Persephone.

Similarly, Lin-Manuel Miranda's groundbreaking concert-turned-recorded musical Hamilton also bends the truth to provide a modern and hipster version of the American founding fathers. Making national heroes into a tragic Greek chorus is significant to understand that Miranda's mythic reinterpretation focuses on clichéd structures because these ideas still hold the viewers in the grip on a visceral level.

What has remained relevant in myths is what appears to retain the possibilities for continuous renewal throughout each artistic medium. The characters, the hero's search and the struggle between gods and monsters which are part of the mythos are just as meaningful to the reader, the viewer, and the listener of the contemporary world. This hunger for the grandiose of escapist settings and heroic ventures appears to be as ravenous as ever in the disjoined and disconnected twenty-first century.

However, as soon as we speak of contemporary myth adaptations, it is immediately evident that these works perform much more than mere entertainment and the recreation of the old myths. The best of these reinventions bring fresh ways of understanding to stories that have the timelessness that ensures they will never get stale. Subsequently future creators and viewers can keep on drinking from these bottomless mythic troughs – and decode truths of the deepest significance hidden in simplest of escapisms. That as the cultures evolve and technologies improve, mythology is and always will be the timeless art of telling stories.

Illustrative Examples

Myths can be considered as folklore which is a ubiquitous part of people's experience with myths and legends being semiotizations of the principal concerns of various populations at different stages of development of different societies of the world and different time periods. These stories employ those figures and topics, in relation to which people can find themselves and which stem from humanity's dream, suffering, and struggle. In this Unit it will be possible to focus on the selected examples of such myths and legends as well as the main archetypes in myths today and in the distant past – The Trickster, The Hero and the Femme Fatale.

Clowns are created since the beginning of time as creatures that disrupt social order, roles, reality, and associated fun as well. Very often male, the trickster is a wandering being, a being of mixed origins that acts undercover and whose goal does not lie in the control of a population as is the case of the so called werewolf. They are tough and complex personalities who relish turning over the conventional law and order within the mere intent to dissect the vice in human nature. Thus, in spite of disorder, the tricksters make that truth can be laid bare or that environments or characters are prepared for it.

Loki the Norse god and coyote spirit from Native America myths can be considered to be the most outstanding characters who are tricksters. Loki also has the characteristic of being cunning and a pest to other gods of the Aesir and he is depicted as always searching for ways of picking quarrels for purposes of fun. However, he also activated the processes that led to the occurrence of events that would introduce renewal. Similarly, Scheiermacher's Native American legends where the coyote figure is almost always indulging in some prohibited or prohibited resource, his faults assist the viewers to gain something about the world. One other character related to intelligence and shrewdness is the spider associated with Anansi, the West African supreme god of trickery who gets food, money, power, and a position through trickery. Knowledge as well as love are depicted in Anansi's stories and the evil aspect of greed is also shown even in a hero and it will not let the hero see the bigger picture.

Thus, the 'Trickster' did not retreat from the stage of the mass media, but merely transformed the role and significance which it performed in the modern world. For instance, the main adversary from Batman's show, the Joker, insistently incites conflicts and combats in order to gain control over persons and to avenge oneself. Marvel Comics also portray Loki as complex villain who has plans that are interwoven with the heroes' when it is convenient for schemes motivated by malevolence with aspiration to power.

Hero myths come with the theme of having a hero whose main role is to leave normal life and embark on a great and perilous journey. They come back a changed person, bearing blessings and with information that they pass to society. Hero tales therefore symbolise the map of life development and self-actualisation.

This is because the greatest possible support, before the start of the hero's journey, is when a structure is put in place. It starts with 'call to adventure,' that is when distress comes looking for the hero and he/she answers the call. He overcomes foes and adversaries, learns new and improved ways of doing things and acquires new and improved friends and controls enemies and barriers and succeeds in the ultimate climactic Ordeal in which victory is earned at the very last possible second. Casting tactics aims at enlightening the hero with new knowledge then the hero vanishes to the community to share with experiences that intends to affect the society positively.

In this formula of monomyth, it depicts many of the basic steps that are used to create the mythos heroic archetypes. In the Mesopotamian epic, Gilgamesh which tells the story of the great flood, the protagonist Gilgamesh ventures out of his city to conquer the fierce world and become immortal after the death of his friend Enkidu. He too, to face all these dangers emerges as a survivor and conforms with the laws of life and finally goes home to become a better monarch and a ruler.

The most recognised and perhaps the earliest tale of hero journey is in the epic called the odyssey by Homer. Last but not the least, after many years of bloody wars and battles, the great epic ten years' voyage of Odysseus begins and the adversaries he has to face are Charybdis the terrible whirlpool and Scylla, the rock of the six heads. Even though he outsmarts the creatures and fights the mythical beasts to become a king again, the man finds his family after the threats are defeated and the suitors are vanquished.

The following are the elements of the mythic structure of hero narratives used in contemporary hero legends: Similarly in Star Wars there is young man Luke Skywalker who at first rebels against the call for being the hero of destiny obeys his wise preceptor Obi-Wan Kenobi and joins mastery of the force for combating the evil organization the Galactic Empire. In the same way, the series of books intends the story of Harry Potter, an orphan and a magical growing in Hogwarts School of Witchcraft. In turn, Harry finds himself exposed to the malicious deeds of the murderous wizard, Voldemort together with friends Hermione and Ron being made gradually braver and more powerful for the forces of light in every film.

From fertility the earth mother, Inanna Kali, and Artemis are the femme fatalities in Greek myths Sirens Scylla and Medusa deceive men with their desirable beauty but with the intent to kill. The sirens sang to the sailors and invited the boys to come closer to death or to get carnal knowledge, which is represented by lust. With Siren Medusa making men who were attracted to her beauty turn into stone, the first message of love is that it can incapacitate.

This meaning asserts the theme of vampires as the sexual liberation and the mutilation of the gender roles. They personify the tragic shoot of forbidden passion that seduces men away from their responsibilities and then lets them die. The erasure of desire within the film's femme fatale elucidates the regenerative power of this more virile figure and triumphant obliterating of submerged matriarchal barbarity in the name of societal health.

The sexual predator model of the femme fatale persists in various forms in the post-World War II cultures, especially in the Hollywood film noir. Here, spider women like Kathie from Out of the Past are also evidence of female deceit and untrustworthiness of the vamps, moll dolls, and sirens to betray. Quentin Tarantino also infused the type with Lucy Liu's vengeful Tokyo yakuza O-Ren Ishii in Kill Bill as well as with Zoë Bell's bounty-hunting sidekicks to Stuntman Mike in

Deathproof. It is not only films that depict lethal glamour, but also singers, such as Lana Del Rey, embody today's version of the mujer fatal, the deadly woman.

Heroes and mythologies give the cultural ever-enduringness to the global axiological values and immortals with the help of bright characters and simple narratives. Cunning figures, knights and seductresses remain essential motifs inspiring archetypal dramatic action in life revealing itself in the course of human existence. While specifics would vary, these tales and their heroes, undoubtedly, will remain meaningful and significant to the continuous construction of meaning through storytelling by people as long as legends speak to existence's dreams and dread.

Contemporary Mythology

It is worth noting that storytelling has been in people's lifestyle for many years; those being; urban myths or fables. These are in fact mostly quasi-mythological stories that include important functions in the society, such as ethical and didactic ones. Nowadays many traditions of the folk culture are not left without a secondary and carry on their fulfillment many functions of folklore, but not without some changes following the innovation of the new technologies and integration of the world.

Hence, the growth of urban legends pertains interest and fears that people have and sheds light on various facets of the human mind. It is one thing to be scared of something but it is quite a different thing to be scared because something out of the norm has occurred, today stories of horrors, dangerous strangers, and strange happenings which used to circulate in the mouths of people circulate in the internet. This process makes it easy through the help of the internet; these stories undergo a process of evolving up to the point that they are new unique stories. Details could, therefore, change, but this is the nature of the genre because every genre satisfies some primary or secondary needs, fears, and questions that people have.

There is also the ability to explain new narratives of contemporary life that might engage archetypes that are essential to the human condition. Adultery and other stories between celebrities and other things that are considered off-limits, as well as other topics that pertain to matters that are regarded as invasions of privacy of different personalities, form more contemporary examples of folklore. There is also the comparison in other creepy and villainous scripts, the supernatural and celebrities' sexual misconducts. However, it suffices to see these new components emerging at the surface of this culture to emerge with conclusions opposite to what the theme suggests: these stories appear rather stereotyped if one examines them carefully and pull them at their roots; these create images that recall classical archetypes such as good and evil, the mysterious, the protagonists and villains.

The presence of these tales in the modern word and the fact that people continue to listen to them implies that there are fundamental needs that are being fulfilled in this place. Hunt for stimulation involves following what is weird and scary to people in a bid to catch the excitement of performing acts of Individual filth. If you meet confirmation of your absurd perceptions about the reality, then everything is okay. Morality tales reinforce values. This is because, due to the pliable nature of modern folklore these myths can resonate with the modern man even as they shed their time relevance. People come to the hearth of the World Wide Web of the technological world of the twenty-first century to watch the dreams and phobias that became the everyday stories.

Regarding the urban legends it is important to state today's mythologies, which are produced and shared by modern fandoms using additional narratives in various fictions and growing limited cultures of the given fan groups. Once restricted to particular and often very particular niches, fandoms have evolved into one of the crucial facets of the popular culture and popular mythology.

This feature is essentially an open-write setting that allows the followers of books, movies, video games and anything else that is considered entertaining to write their own stories in the shared fictional world. As for this part, fans discuss new myths and themes that have not been disclosed in the main mythologies and the participatory extension of myths serves this issue as a fulfillment of the fans' needs. The works described in the NDA context contain hot themes, such as romance, sexuality, ethnic or other minorities, and other themes the readers of NDA do not want to be associated with.

These other mythologies can therefore make change to impact on the mainstream appreciation of such ideas. In this regard, it can be assumed that through the provision of equal attention to sexual minorities and the creation of an environment in which homosexual pairings are allowed in fan fiction, the transition to a progressive position in politics of sexuality and identity was stimulated. So the passion of the audiences has also delivered in stopping shows from being cancelled before time and also in getting shows that are spin offs and revivals demanding to be different from the original. The exchange is mutual, that is the text calls for a response from the fans and the fans' response affects the text.

Besides fan fiction, fans have their own Rule 34 and create a set of customs, a vocabulary, rituals, and objects that are considered as holy. Stakeholder activities become legend, and fan meetings in their turn become rites. Slang and memes are encultured signifiers because they are prone to contain inside jokes that fans of the show would immediately pick up on. The personages from the legends transform into the symbols of the faith or cult images of sects.

Thus, the fans return the commercial properties into the elements of legends that are as significant as the classical gods and heroes or legendary characters. The passion-time combination of the directors/singers/artists results in their invented personalities that have lives and myths which fill up the society. Last but not least, passion of fandoms allows an influence the real-world the imaginary with concepts of beliefs and norms – the evidence of humanity's primary focus on myth.

These are the incorporations of new mythology in an optimistic folkloristic change and the fans' culture that outline the directions of mythology in the globalized and technopolized universe. So will our myths, for as the over-informing web of links appends to the global pool of collected experience and apercu, so will the tentacles of connection.

It is vital to acknowledge technology as a phenomenon that exists outside already participating in the process of transfer and metamorphosis of myths as they cross over to another form. But possibly even more as those social phenomena which activity is progressively enabled by advancements in technology: virtual reality and artificial intelligence trigger metaphysical questions which are hard to answer without referring to mythology. With the help of tools that look like magic the human race keeps building reality and in so doing, our stories stir promises of technologies beyond our imagination from the concepts of envisioning to fearing an apocalyptic future.

Myths also help cultures to come to terms with how different they are in the contemporary globally diverse society. When globalization sets the intermediate stage for two histories, the histories harmoniously interweave and enrich each other. Thus, the society, being dominant, succeeds in painting over the cultural models of minorities in black and white, the minorities, in turn, respond with myths of rebellion. Accordingly, fictions of the immigrants become myths and, at the same time, function as the grounds for signalling about conspiracies of the top officials and create a collective focus fear.

Therefore, it can be concluded that mythology as a specific type of the storytelling has not lost its significance even through the prism of the technological progress. Who are we? Who do we want to become as an individual? We are scared of turning to be the men that women will not be willing to wed or sleep with, or be the women that men will not be willing to wed or sleep with. Often these were encapsulated into myths crossing the language and geographical barriers. These solutions may have entailed the need to invent new stories that would propagating pluralism, and not tribalism. This mythic rewriting is already noticeable in fandom, oral tradition, and activist perimeters, which resist the conventional and institutionalized roles.

Unlike what some critics presume about thick information overdose being the surest way to eliminate mythology, the world is already globalised and filled with information and mythic imagination cannot go begging. The following decades shall see these mythologies of participation only increase at an exponential rate that will be arrested by digital media due to the nature of its reappropriation. They will mix and merge with other stories and become new inherited ones, out of which some will be stored in the nether of the quickly forgotten while others eternally remain there. As the external facade of mystique, mythology will continue inflexibly to protect and to attend to the people's philosophy, concern and dream in the core.

As to how future myths will emerge is not precisely acutely known Besides, socio cultural impact of future myths is likely to be monumental. Folly and globalization pull the humanity into the uncertain worlds that have to host dragons in threats and opportunities. Luckily, we will have a great deal of myths to help determine something or other and, indeed, to throw a light on the situation.

Glossary and Timeline

Language is another element of mythology that is worth examining; it is rather diverse and abundant. Some notes that explain terms and characters in myths are more than just the companions: they open the door to different civilizations and cultures. Be it gods and spirits or half-gods and other powerful beings or symbols and other objects or other legendary characters, each of the terms is highly valuable and active with so many semantics. For example when we are speaking of Zeus or even Odin or Anansi we are not simply speaking about the protagonists in novels; rather we are evoking people's culture and their moral standards. They represent the pillars of power, knowledge, and scheming; leading the definitions of right and wrong besides contributing to the structure of society.

Through the study of such terms and figures, the viewer is introduced to a liberal perspective of the human psyche and society. Legends can bring into the spotlight primary images that can be found in every culture; for instance, the hero saga, the jokester, and the mother figure. These motifs frame both the spatial and temporal contexts, which means that they touch upon presumably essential aspects of human existence. In a way, mythology is not set in the past; rather, it is an ongoing process in which past myths are adopted as one's identity and turned into contemporary myths in literature and movies.

It is also important how these narratives are set in historical prospective other than knowing the vocabulary of mythology. This means that the depiction of a timeline of different ancient mythologies makes it easy to do a comparison of the stories and to note the various changes that occurred between different stories. As one examines the timeline starting from the origins of Mesopotamia up to the Homeric epics of Greece and the philosophical foundations of the Indian traditions, one equally notes the variegation and the similarities of the human storytelling modes. That is why this theory focuses on how inhabitants of various civilizations affected and evolved their myths based on the corresponding environment, technologies, and interculturally.

These examples from the historical panorama make us remember the idea about mythology as a set of images, which is not invariable, but variable and developing. The fact is that the reception of myths can be culturally transformed as due to newly emerged discoveries, social processes, and, finally, the dialogue between cultures. Recognizing these changes might be helpful when studying the patterns of how societies reinvent themselves after adversities or changes, be they natural disasters, wars, or revolutions in thought processes. The mythological stories are with us, though the meanings attached to them evolve to fit the current generations.

In addition, general subjectivity and focusing on mythology performs as highly significant contribution in the modern society struggling with questions about its identification, values, and purpose. Since cultural differences came close due to globalization, mythology is a way to integrate new culture with people's respect to it. It balances with the other type of thinking in that it engages different ways of seeing the world and makes us appreciate the complexity of life. In other words, while a myth itself divulges information about the ancestry, purpose, and perception of a specific culture, it also calls for the identification of the shared features of both global and local humanity.

As the present edition will provide the readers with the definitions of mythological terms and the list of mythological characters, as well as the timeline of the histories of ancient mythologies, the main purpose of the present work is to encourage people to discuss the meanings of the myths nowadays.

As a result, the thirst of the myths invites the reader into the ancient world, providing an opportunity to reflect on a widely known, yet often neglected story. Lastly, the narratives that we discover in turn help to recall such wisdom that it raises the importance of stories for our identities and for our ethical perceptions of life, thus pointing out directions to the mysterious maze of human life. They say that archaeology is the science that allows one not only to look at the past but also in it and see what was needed to create the present The time has come to use this opportunity and, moreover, elucidate the importance and the chance to make connections that will lead to the future.

Mythological glossary

Greek Mythology

Zeus: The king of the gods which is sometimes depicted as the sky and thunder.

Hera: aka the great mother and the divine regent, who was worshipped as the queen of heavens and the patroness of marriage.

Apollo: This includes; the sun god, the god of light, god of music and, the god of prophecy.

Artemis: As the moon, the huntress and the master of beasts.

Athena: The Latin goddess of wisdom and the goddess of crafts and warfare.

Hades: The Greek term or the name for the god of the underworld.

Poseidon: The god of sea, earthquake or the foces of nature, and horses.

Heroes: The characters such as Heracles, Perseus, and Odysseus who have done incredible things during the Greek mythology.

Titans: A race of men, which presided over the unruly parts of the earth before the Olympians were placed in power.

The Trojan War: Legendary fight of Greeks with the Trojans, that took place in ancient times.

Norse Mythology

Odin: Lede; all-father god of the wise, warriors and the dead.

Thor: The deity associated with thunder, power and might and the protector of the people.

Loki: The clever, mischievous deity, which more often than not exploits folly.

Freya: The Venus: goddess of love, beauty and fertility.

Ragnarök: Judgment day, the struggle between 'good' and 'evil', when people meet their gods face to face.

Yggdrasil: The significant Jötnar Yggdrasil that unites all the nine spheres of the Norse universe.

Jötnar: Titans or adversaries most of the time of the gods.

Valkyries: Daughters personifying the souls of female warriors who select those warriors to be taken to Valhalla.

Einherjar: Odin's chosen warriors who are expected to accompany him during the end of the world-Ragnarok.

Midgard: The sphere of people.

Egyptian Mythology

Ra: Re, the sun god who was represented as a falcon or a man with a falcon's head.

Isis: He wife of Wadjet, protector of women in childbirth and the gods of Lower Egypt.

Osiris: This god is associated with the domains of the underworld, resurrection as well as fertility.

Horus: The sky god represented either by a falcon or a man with a falcon headed figure at times.

Anubis: Osiris: the god of dead who is at times represented by a jackal or a man wearing the head of the animal.

Ma'at: The goddess of truth, justice, order and cosmic law and justice.

Set: The storm and desert deity of chaos.

The Book of the Dead: Syllabus of spells and texts to assist the deceased to use while in the after world.

The Pyramid Texts: Pre-colonial religions which belong to some of the oldest religious texts and can still be traced in pyramid of the Egypt.

The Ennead: A group of nine gods of the Heliolatric cult.

Other Mythologies

Anansi: One from West African folklore who is sometimes represented by a spider.

Coyote: A wise character of the tales of Native Americans; a legendary clever man.

Kitsune: From Japanese mythology, it is a fox spirit which is depicted as a trickster character.

Shiva: It is one of the Hindu gods mainly referred to as the god of destruction and regeneration.

Krishna: The male deity loved by women, the god of affection, mercy as well as knowledge in Hindu Mythology.

The Dreamtime: An idea derived from the Aboriginal Australians' legends, signifying the time in which the creation happened.

The Rainbow Serpent: Refers to a god which is a figure from the Australian Aboriginal mythology.

Quetzalcoatl: A god of the Aztec people who is patron of the wind and the patron of the schools and of artists.

The Monkey King: The Chinese trickster god famous for his escapades and pranks.

The Mahabharata: A sacred Indic book containing the Bhagavad Gita which informs part of the Mahabharata.

Ancient Mythologies Timeline

Greek Mythology

8th Century BCE: Homer composes the Iliad as well as the Odyssey.

7th Century BCE: Speaking about the Ancient Greek authors, Hesiod composes Theogony and Works and Days.

5th Century BCE: Aeschylus, Sophocles and Euripides are playwrights who deal in mytholological tragedies.

4th Century BCE: Myths are depicted in philosophical analysis through works of Plato and Aristotle.

Norse Mythology

9th Century CE: There are distant accounts of the Viking age, which disseminated the Norse mythology across the continent.

10th Century CE: The collection of Old Norse poems named The Poetic Edda is created.

13th Century CE: About 1220 AD, Snorri Sturluson composes a sort of manual on the mythology of northern heathendom.

Egyptian Mythology

3100 BCE: The formal integration of the Egypt's Two Kingdoms to become one political entity referred to as the Pharaonic period.

2600 BCE: The history of its writing can be understood based on the location where the Pyramid Texts are inscribed which is in the pyramids of the Old Kingdom.

1550 BCE: The publication of the Book of the Dead starts to appear in funerary processes.

1300 BCE: The New Kingdom specifically the Amarna Period when Akhenaten is commanding the people to pray to Aten.

Other Mythologies

2000 BCE: The first known forms of the story of the Mahabharata and the Ramayana originally originate from the Indian subcontinent.

1000 BCE: Zhou Dynasty in china also the period that the mythological productions and storytelling are documented.

500 BCE: This paper presents the Aeneid as a Roman piece by Virgil is well, which is a work of the historical epic drawn from the Greco-Roman myths.

1000 CE: ThePopolVuh, Mayan mythology is a compilation of myths.

1500 CE: The Aztec Empire at its peak or rather the classic period or the empire's golden age has a splendid mythology.

1800 CE: European settlers document the Dreamtime stories about myths of Australian Aboriginal people.

Finally, myths and legends cannot be limited to reception history as they are still influencing today culture and people's view upon the world. Such knowledge increases our awareness of the variation in people's stories and the similarities of belonging to humanity.

It must therefore be understood that myths and legends are not history and relics of the past, but are in fact very much a part of the present and the continuous history of the world. These works help to save and cultivate the identity, and deliver understanding of the essence of the man which does not depend on time and the space. Focusing on the general concepts, it can be stated that myths serve as a source of guidance through modern living conditions that represent such a significant value since the contemporary world is characterized by constant development and increased interconnectedness.

As such, mythography is an exploration of the ethnopsychological reality of culture and a step into the minds of people. To me, these stories are about the things that humans are afraid of and the things which they dream about that make people recall their common denominator. In doing so, one cannot deny the fact, that as we engage with these narratives we not only remember the past, but make present and future a richer and better place.

Regardless of specified cultural beliefs in myths and legends, they are a great uniting factor in a world that has become hostile and segregated. They challenge us to the underlying fact that even though we are absolutely different, we are not absolutely different. Thus, recognizing and valuing such tales, we are capable of promoting the viewers' enhanced level of empathy and, therefore, mutual understanding.

Looking into the future humanities still holds an important place elucidated through myths and legends. Regardless of whether they are a new type of narration or a new reading of the legends, people will go on touching, awakening, encouraging, and upsetting. Everything that has been said above proves that the study of myths and legends is not just the scholarly occupation, it is human values discovery and furthering of intercultural understanding for the benefit of everyone.

Thus, the values that myths and legends depict are important in order to be closer to the past, to understand the present and to define the future. They are the ultimate fabric of human existence and a constant indication of individual and collective memory of mankind. This way, as we listen to these stories, we pay respect to the adages and at the same time – become the authors of the contemporary history.

Disclaimer

Everything shared in this book should be considered as educational and informative in nature. The author and publisher shall not be responsible for any loss or damage suffered by any reader directly or indirectly through reading of, reliance on, and use of information that only the author and the publisher know at the time of writing this book.

Some of the suggestions given and the approaches recommended in the book may not be applicable to certain circumstances. The author and the publisher shall not be held responsible for any damages caused as a direct result of the use or non-use of the information presented in this book.

It is understood that readers should not rely on it for professional solicitations such as medical, legal, financial, and other related opinions. If any professional help is needed, then advice of a competent professional person should be taken.

The author and the publisher will not be held responsible for direct, indirect, special, or consequential damages or any other costs whatsoever arising from the use of the information present herein in this book.

About the Author

Maher Asaad Baker (In Arabic: ماهر أسعد بكر), is a Syrian musician, author, journalist, VFX & graphic artist, and director. He was born in Damascus in 1977. He grew up with a dream of being one of the most well-known artists in the world, and he has been working hard to achieve it ever since.

He started his career in 1997 when he was only 20 years old. He had a passion for technology and media, and he taught himself how to develop applications and websites. He also explored various types of media-creating paths, such as music production, graphic design, video editing, animation, and filmmaking. He was not satisfied with just being a consumer of media; he wanted to be a creator of media.

Reading was another source of inspiration for him. He was always surrounded by books as a child, thanks to his father's extensive library. He read books from different genres, topics, and perspectives. He read books for knowledge, for wisdom, for entertainment, for enlightenment. Reading stimulated his imagination and curiosity. Reading also developed his writing skills.

He did not start writing professionally until later in his life, as he was busy with other projects and pursuits. But when he did start writing, he proved himself to be a talented and prolific writer. He wrote articles for various newspapers and magazines on topics such as politics, culture, society, art, technology, and more. He wrote books that were informative and insightful. He wrote books that were creative and captivating. He wrote books that were best-selling and award-winning.

He is most known for his book "How I wrote a million Wikipedia articles", where he shares his experience of being one of the most prolific contributors to the online encyclopedia. He reveals his methods, techniques, strategies, and secrets of writing high-quality articles on any subject in record time. He also discusses the benefits and challenges of being a Wikipedia editor in the age of information overload.

He is also known for his novel "Becoming the man", where he tells the story of a young man who goes through a series of transformations in his life. The novel explores themes such as identity, masculinity, self-discovery, love, loss, and redemption. The novel is based on his journey to becoming who he is today.

Copyright © 2024 Maher Asaad Baker